IMAGES
of America

NORTHWEST
AIRLINES
THE FIRST EIGHTY YEARS

Colonel Louis.H. Brittin (1877–1952) founded Northwest Airways in 1926. He achieved his dream of seeing his airline establish air services from Minneapolis/St. Paul to the Pacific Northwest (Seattle) on December 3, 1933. He resigned from Northwest in 1934.

(*cover*) Speedway Field—later Wold Chamberlain Field and now Minneapolis/St. Paul International Airport—is seen in 1926 in front of Northwest Airways' first wooden hangar. In the white flying suit is Charles "Speed" Holman, one of Northwest's first pilots and its first operations manager. Holman had already become a legend in Minnesota and other parts of the U.S. in the 1920s for his air racing triumphs and aerobatic exhibitions. The aircraft is an early Northwest Airways Laird LC-B "Commercial" (C240) and the two other characters are T.K. Kelly, described as a "Twin Cities advertising mogul," and Kelly's assistant.